CW00828940

Lizzie Cornwall

365 DAYS OF INSPIRATION

Copyright © Summersdale Publishers Ltd, 2012

All rights reserved.

No part of this book may be reproduced by any means, nor transmitted, nor translated into a machine language, without the written permission of the publishers.

Condition of Sale
This book is sold subject to the condition that it shall not, by way of trade or otherwise, be lent, re-sold, hired out or otherwise circulated in any form of binding or cover other than that in which it is published and without a similar condition including this condition being imposed on the subsequent publisher.

Summersdale Publishers Ltd
46 West Street
Chichester
West Sussex
PO19 1RP
UK

www.summersdale.com

Printed and bound in the Czech Republic

ISBN: 978-1-84953-331-7

Substantial discounts on bulk quantities of Summersdale books are available to corporations, professional associations and other organisations. For details contact Nicky Douglas by telephone: +44 (0) 1243 756902, fax: +44 (0) 1243 786300 or email: nicky@summersdale.com.

To Gen -
Our special inspiration
From Mummy + Daddy
31/5/14

Luv U, darling plum (see 8th June) you have your single step taken.
from Dad.
to ~~[illegible]~~ my Deerest Dorter.

JANUARY

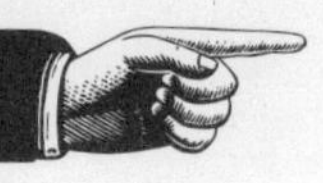

New Year's Day: Start a journal and make a conscious effort to write in it every day, either as soon as you wake up, when you get home or just before you go to bed. Include details that strike you as interesting.

Forget the cold, the ice and the dark evenings – wrap yourself up, get outside and do something you would usually never do at this time of year.

Join a yoga or t'ai chi class – both will help you be physically stronger, mentally calmer and better prepared to face the challenges of the year ahead.

Prepare a meal using only seasonal produce – beetroot, kale, turnips, pears, tangerines, chestnuts, venison, guinea fowl and oysters are all great at this time of year.

Invent a new word (one that sounds at least slightly plausible!) and try to use it as much as possible to see if other people pick it up.

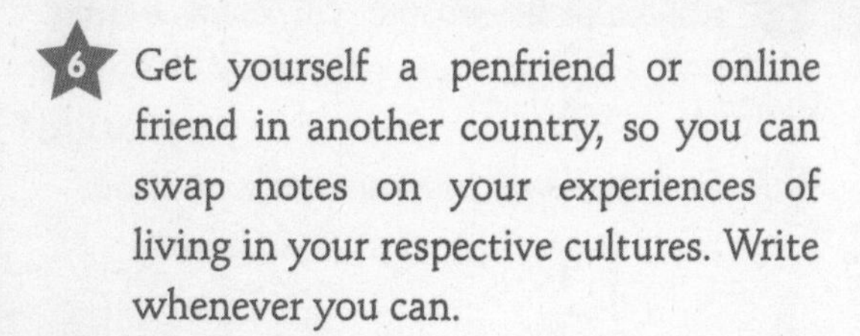

6 Get yourself a penfriend or online friend in another country, so you can swap notes on your experiences of living in your respective cultures. Write whenever you can.

7 Take a different route to work, and take special notice of your new surroundings.

8 Laugh as much as possible today. Ask everyone you see to tell you their favourite joke, or go to see a live stand-up show.

Revisit a book or film that held particular significance for you as a child.

Consider one of your daily routines – could it be improved? If so, how?

Go into your garden or local park, pick a tree and draw it in as much detail as possible. Make a date to revisit the tree in spring, summer and autumn and record how it's changed by drawing it again.

Look up something you have never quite understood, or have always wanted to know more about.

Catch the trade wind in your sails. Explore. Dream. Discover.

Mark Twain

Imagination will take you everywhere.

Albert Einstein

Find a local craft class and sign up for a sculpting, woodwork or glass blowing course – anything that grabs you.

Cut out 'must' and 'have to' from your vocabulary for the day. Replace them with 'I'd love to' or 'I can't wait to' – even if it's 'I can't *wait* to do the washing up!'

Document your day in photos. Whether it's just the everyday stuff or something special, try to see the beauty in whatever you do.

Sign up now to take part in a charity run, walk or skydive later in the year, and start preparing for it.

Make papier mâché models of some winter birds, such as robins, blue tits, wrens and goldfinches, and paint them to display in your home.

Listen to a genre of music that's out of your usual comfort zone. You could borrow CDs from your local library or listen to music online.

Dig out an old board game (or go hunting for one in a charity shop) and invite some friends around to play.

Write a haiku about snow.

Buy a beer- or wine-making kit and see if you can concoct a delicious drop of hooch to keep you warm on these cold evenings.

Watch your favourite programme on television then, straight away, start writing a sequel to the episode. Even if it's a game show, make it as dramatic as possible.

Buy a children's colouring book and a pack of crayons. Spend half an hour colouring in and don't worry about staying inside the lines!

Imagine you have just won the jackpot in the Lottery. Write a dream list of all the things you'd do with your new fortune.

JANUARY

To do a dull thing with style – now that's what I call art.

Charles Bukowski

The man who removes a mountain begins by carrying away small stones.

Chinese proverb

National Puzzle Day: Buy yourself a Rubik's Cube – and master it.

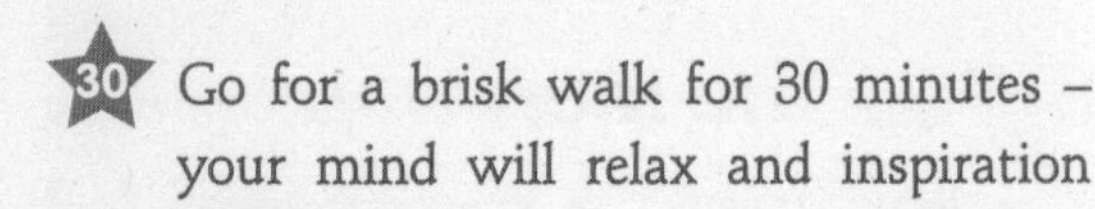

Go for a brisk walk for 30 minutes – your mind will relax and inspiration will come!

Listen to talk radio and write down all the important points that are discussed – consider your stance on each of them.

FEBRUARY

Visit your local church, temple, mosque or synagogue. Even if you are not religious, or belong to a different faith, take the time to appreciate the architecture and the atmosphere of a place of worship.

Buy a magazine or newspaper you would never usually consider. It's good to get a new perspective on things from time to time.

Draw your hand. Put in every line you can see, even if this means it looks more like a ball of string than a hand!

Leave your TV, laptop and mobile phone turned off all afternoon. Spend your time absorbing the sights, smells and sounds of your neighbourhood.

Volunteer a few hours of your time to a charity shop or homeless shelter, and strike up friendly conversations with all the people you meet.

Close your eyes and imagine yourself waking up in five years' time. What does your room look like? Are you alone or with someone? What do you wear? Use these images to spur you on to attain your goals.

Teach yourself to touch-type. It will make writing your first novel that much faster!

Make a playlist or a CD for someone, full of all the music you think they will love but haven't discovered yet. Really put thought into the content and the order of the songs.

Nothing really matters except what you do now in this instant of time.

Eileen Caddy

Happiness is a way of travel, not a destination.

Roy M. Goodman

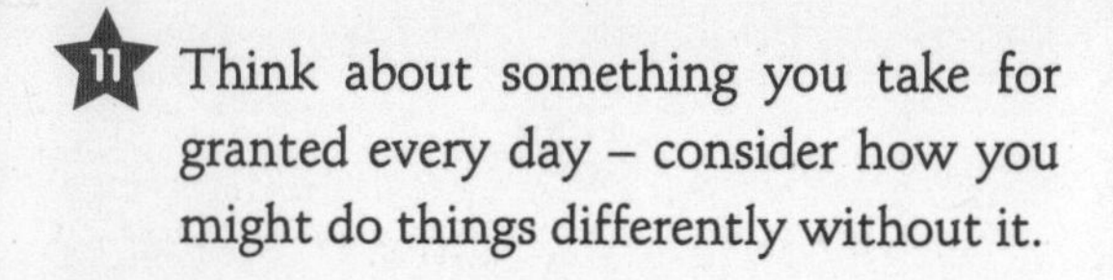

11 Think about something you take for granted every day – consider how you might do things differently without it.

12 Find an art print, photo or poster that really inspires you, frame it yourself and put it in a place where you will see it often.

13 Draw up some basic plans for redecorating a room in your house. Make a list of ideal decor and draw up a floor plan. Once you have your ideas together, look into how to get the work done and take the first steps to transforming your living space.

Valentine's Day: Give someone special a bunch of red roses with a single white rose in the centre, with a note saying 'You stand out from the crowd'.

Read your favourite poem aloud. You absorb things in a different way when you speak or listen.

Create a quirky sculpture out of spare bits and pieces you have lying around – make it as elaborate as possible.

Embrace your passions. Whatever it is you feel really strongly about, or whatever your talent – share it with others today. Spread your knowledge and enthusiasm.

Write a poem about a famous historical figure you admire.

Spend an hour or so browsing your favourite social networking site, to see what interesting things people are up to.

Plant a tree in memory of someone that was close to you.

Introduce yourself to a neighbour – preferably bearing baked goodies!

Stop what you are doing and take a half-hour nap. Your mind continues to work subconsciously while you sleep, so when you wake up, you may just be surprised with an unexpected 'Eureka!' moment.

Read 'If' by Rudyard Kipling.

Be not simply good, be good for something.

Henry David Thoreau

Luck is a dividend of sweat. The more you sweat, the luckier you get.

Ray Kroc

Choose an album that's been reviewed in this week's paper and go out and buy or download it. Really listen to it.

Create your own style by designing and making a T-shirt print. Use card to create a template and apply the design to a blank shirt using fabric paint.

Fill a whole page of a notebook with doodles. Draw whatever comes to mind.

Leap Day: Consider this a 'bonus day' and use your extra 24 hours to do some good in the world.

MARCH

Visit your nearest live music venue and buy tickets to see whoever is playing this week.

Buy some fresh flowers for your home – they'll add colour and life to the room and your mind.

Go down to your local train station or park and spend an hour people-watching.

People often say that motivation doesn't last. Well, neither does bathing – that's why we recommend it daily.

Zig Ziglar

Always be a first-rate version of yourself, instead of a second-rate version of someone else.

Judy Garland

Think of the silliest thing you could do right now. Do it.

Write as many sentences as you can to do with the colour black.

Take a bus ride to somewhere you've never been before (just make sure you check the timetable, so you can get back!).

Call a family member that you don't speak to very often, and find out what they've been up to.

Go outside and smell the fresh air. Take deep breaths and really notice everything you can about its smell. Now come back inside and try to describe it – in prose, poem or painting.

Find a tasty recipe and cook a vegan meal for your friends or family.

Ask a musical friend to give you a lesson on their instrument. Aim to learn at least one simple song.

Search for the most shocking, outrageous piece of art you can find in a museum of modern art or on the Internet.

Play 'Just a Minute' – try to talk for 60 seconds on one topic without hesitating or repeating any words except the subject words.

World Sleep Day: Find some tranquillity by enhancing the peacefulness of your bedroom. Invest in some blackout blinds, ear plugs, a luxurious mattress or anything else that will make each night's sleep perfect.

Invent a new sandwich using your favourite foods. Once you've created your culinary masterpiece, invite some friends over and make it for them.

Design your own stained-glass window and construct it using cellophane and craft paper.

Write out, by hand, your favourite passage from a great book, or something you've read today that strikes you as powerful. Using a pen and paper will help you connect with the message.

Create a cartoon strip to illustrate your day.

First Day of Spring: Celebrate by eating your breakfast outside – put an umbrella up if it's raining!

Plan and book a weekend in the great outdoors.

Give meditation a try – it can be as simple as sitting comfortably in peaceful surroundings and being aware of your breathing, in and out, in an effort to clear your mind of all thoughts.

Practise contour drawing: sit in front of a mirror and draw your face, without looking down at the piece of paper.

Organise a book-swap club. Everybody brings along a number of unwanted books, and you can take away as many as you came with!

Wake up ten minutes earlier than usual and stretch every major muscle in your body. If you can, find a set of stretches to follow. It'll set you up for a great day.

Life begins at the end of your comfort zone.

Neale Donald Walsch

Ever tried. Ever failed. No matter. Try again. Fail again. Fail better.

Samuel Beckett

Create a feature wall in a room of your house that is overdue for redecoration. Choose one strong, bold colour or wallpaper that really expresses your personality.

Set goals to complete over the coming week: complete one sketch per day, write 1,000 words per day, cook with one new ingredient per day – whatever takes your fancy.

Try preparing a special dessert to give yourself a well-deserved treat.

Read *The Seven Habits of Highly Effective People* by Steven Covey, or *How to Win Friends and Influence People* by Dale Carnegie. Even better – read both! Put their points into action.

APRIL

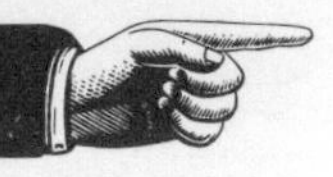

April Fool's Day: Cut out a picture of the lower part of a face (preferably with amusing features) and stick to the bottom of a friend's mug. When they drink from it, everyone will laugh – and they won't know why!

Organise a visit to your nearest real-ale brewery and try one of the unique tipples on offer there!

Start a page of a notebook to write down funny words that amuse you: 'flibbertigibbet' or 'nincompoop', for example. Don't forget to keep topping up the list.

Volunteer to walk a friend's dog, or to walk the dogs at your local shelter. Being around animals naturally relieves stress and cleanses the mind.

Think of a piece of clothing or an outfit that makes you feel good about yourself. Why not have more of the same? Make room in your wardrobe by donating the clothes you never wear to charity.

Find out what you're afraid of and go live there.

Chuck Palahniuk

Genius is one per cent inspiration, ninety-nine per cent perspiration.

Thomas Edison

Embrace those April showers and your inner child: splash paint onto thick watercolour paper, then hold it outside briefly for the elements to work their magic. Use the colourful paper as the background for an art project.

Take arty photos of some of your favourite objects and put them together in a scrap book.

Find a news story that interests you. Try to imagine you are the central person in the story and write an entry of their diary which covers the newsworthy event.

Plant tomato or salad-leaf seeds in pots to keep on your windowsill. In a few weeks you'll be creating some delicious salads!

Decorate the first page of a blank notebook with poems, pictures or doodles. Post it to a friend to fill in page 2 then return it to you. Keep going until the book is full.

Write a letter to someone without using the words 'I', 'me' or 'my'.

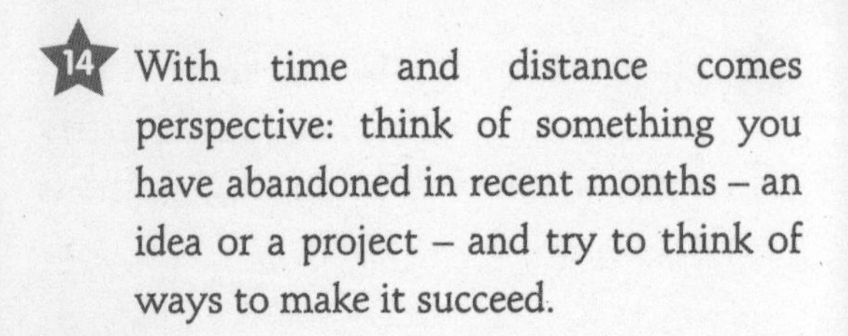

14 With time and distance comes perspective: think of something you have abandoned in recent months – an idea or a project – and try to think of ways to make it succeed.

15 Buy a pack of sculpting clay at your local art or craft shop, and see what you can make.

16 Listen to the sound of rain on your umbrella, and make up a tune to complement it.

Greet everyone you meet today in Continental fashion by kissing them on each cheek.

Find your own mantra and practise repeating it to yourself whenever you feel at a loss. 'I am strong and confident' or 'I am happy and successful' work well!

Energise yourself with a brisk swim – outdoors if possible!

The difference between ordinary and extraordinary is that little extra.

Jimmy Johnson

Necessity is the mother of invention.

Proverb

Earth Day: Collect some stones or shells from a park or beach, and paint them in beautiful colours.

Shakespeare's Birthday: Write a sonnet to the person you care about most in the world. Take a first line from one of Shakespeare's to get you started.

Make a journey in a way you're not used to – take the bus to work, cycle to the pub, take a taxi to a friend's house.

Write an amusing or poignant message on the dirty window of a car or van.

Play the word association game with yourself: write down your starting word and see where you end up.

Pick up a new (good) habit or drop an old (bad) one – for 21 days. This is the length of time it takes to form or lose many habits.

Make a list of all the different jobs you've had. Write about them – your experiences, memories, whether you enjoyed them. Then write about your dream job and compare the accounts.

The best way to predict the future is to create it.

Abraham Lincoln

A mind is like a parachute. It doesn't work if it is not open.

Frank Zappa

MAY

May Day: A spring clean is always a good idea – a clear space is fertile ground for new ideas.

Go to a wildlife sustainability centre and try to pick up ideas about what you could do to help out the birds, bees and other animals in your area.

Dance! For no real reason, wherever you are. Pretend you're in a scene in a musical. You could sing, too, if you like.

Take a sketchbook on the train and see if you can sketch a scene or object just from a fleeting glance.

World Laughter Day (first Sunday in May): Get a group of friends to each write a two-minute stand-up sketch, then throw a comedy night in your front room to laugh the night away!

Make a list of everything you love in life: your favourite songs, great friends, good food, the way your pet smells…

Spend today saying 'yes' to every opportunity that comes along.

Rearrange or redecorate your home workspace – or if you don't have one, create one. It can be anything from a comfy bean bag to a library and bureau – but make sure it suits you.

Take advantage of asparagus season (it's short!). Buy in bulk and make asparagus soup, asparagus and caramelised onion tarts, grilled asparagus with goat's cheese...

Practise the 'Memory Palace' technique (the art of remembering things through mental images) to improve your recall.

Go to a bar alone – be open and act confidently. You're bound to meet some interesting characters or even make new friends!

Compliment everybody you meet on one thing you genuinely like about them.

Get an impromptu haircut – it can revitalise your outlook on life, as well as how you feel about yourself.

Start a nature diary and record all of the plants and animals you come across while out walking (if you don't know the names, take photos and look them up afterwards).

Pay a visit to somewhere you can do brass-rubbing.

Write in recollection and amazement for yourself.

Jack Kerouac

All life is an experiment. The more experiments you make, the better.

Ralph Waldo Emerson

Even if you'll never go through with it, design your dream tattoo.

Buy yourself a hat – the quirkier the better.

Jazz up your kitchen by painting old and faded plates, teapots, biscuit tins or even cupboard doors with crazy patterns.

Plan a cultural trip to Europe – a weekend in Paris, five days in Barcelona – travelling by high-speed train.

Educate yourself on a religion, country or culture you know little about.

Arrange a debate night with some close friends. Bring out the tea and biscuits and discuss a current controversial topic. Do some research first and keep it civil – but make it interesting!

Pick out an object that you find cheerful and draw it using wax crayons or coloured pencils with simple, spontaneous lines.

Take the first step towards something you've always wanted to do, but that has daunted you in the past.

First thing in the morning, write down five reasons why today will be great. Keep the list with you and refer to it throughout the day.

Go to a poetry reading or open-mic night. Even better: volunteer to read a poem or perform one of your own songs.

Take your exercise gear to work and go for a brisk jog on your lunch break. Don't forget the baby wipes, if your workplace doesn't have showers!

Write about your favourite memory of one of your parents.

I have found that if you love life, life will love you back.

Arthur Rubinstein

Be brave. Take risks. Nothing can substitute experience.

Paulo Coelho

JUNE

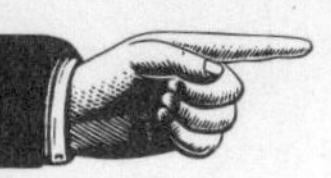

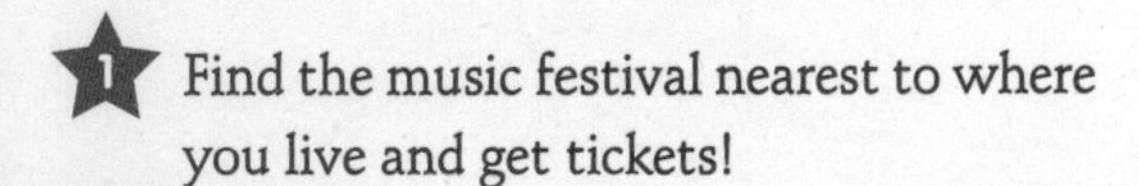

1. Find the music festival nearest to where you live and get tickets!

2. Spend all day actively listening. If you ask somebody how they are, let them say more than 'fine'.

3. Create the wildest outfit you can to wear to work. If your boss won't take offence at skin-tight leopard print and fluorescent tights, go for it!

Keep a notebook and pen next to your bed and record your dreams as soon as you wake up. Get a dream dictionary to interpret their meanings.

Take up a hobby inspired by the Victorian era – cultivate some interestingly shaped facial hair, ride a penny-farthing, have a go at embroidery or candle-wax statuette making.

Start planning Father's Day now – arrange to spend the whole day with your father or father figure and indulge in some of his favourite hobbies.

The world is a book and those who do not travel read only a page.

St Augustine

A journey of a thousand miles begins with a single step.

Lao Tzu

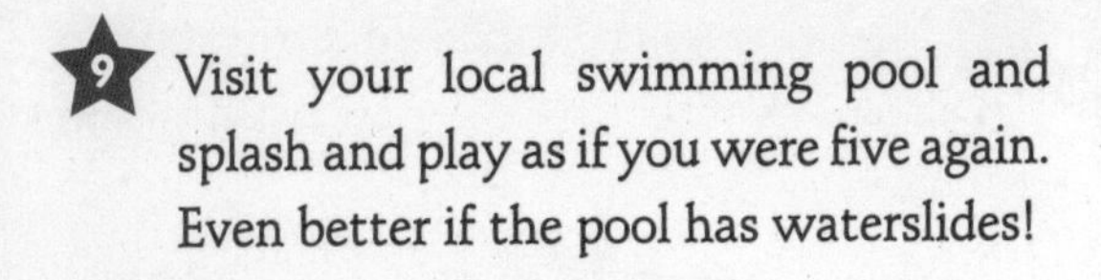

9 Visit your local swimming pool and splash and play as if you were five again. Even better if the pool has waterslides!

10 Volunteer to help out at your local summer fete.

11 Revisit the psychedelic sixties by searching online and listening to some far-out music from that decade – groovy, man.

12 Burn some incense and sit quietly enjoying the aroma. Let your thoughts stray to wherever they want to go.

Visit a museum dedicated to something you have no current interest in – you may be pleasantly surprised.

Make your own crossword using an online puzzle generator. Make the clues personal and send it to friends and family.

Write a letter to someone you've always admired but have never been in contact with.

Select one of your favourite stories and create one or more new characters in the plot – draw or write them into being.

Turn your face to the sun and the shadows fall behind you.

Maori proverb

'Earth' without 'art' is just 'Eh'.

Anonymous

Write down a great memory that made you smile or a joke that made you laugh. Fold up the paper and hide it in the pocket of a jacket you don't always wear to be found in months to come.

Design your own coat of arms, flag or emblem – make it so it reflects your values and personality.

Summer Solstice: Visit a special outdoor spot to watch the sun come up on the longest day of the year.

Listen to a new song on repeat, thinking each time about a different aspect – the rhythm, the lyrics or the melody.

Find an online community for people in your profession. Arrange or attend a social networking event and meet some new people.

Scream at the top of your lungs, punch a pillow as hard as you can, and let yourself go crazy!

Think up five new metaphors or descriptions you think nobody will have ever used before ('This counter is an oryx's horn full of pirouetting shadows').

Take an old coat or jacket and decorate it with badges and patches. If you don't have any badges or patches, start collecting some now!

Find yourself a 'positivity trigger'. This can be anything which has good connotations for you – a key-ring, a photo, or even a small stone or shell you can keep in your pocket, and take out any time you need a boost.

Lie on the grass and watch the sky. See the patterns in the clouds.

Don't judge each day by the harvest you reap but by the seeds that you plant.

Robert Louis Stevenson

If you have built castles in the air, your work need not be lost; that is where they should be. Now put foundations under them.

Henry David Thoreau

JULY

National Motivation Day (UK): Organise a motivational event at work – how about an afternoon of Office Olympics?

Visit a local arts cafe and enjoy soaking up the creative atmosphere as you sip your coffee.

Think about someone in your life you respect and admire – what could you learn from them?

Go back in time and seek some ancient wisdom from the Buddhist text *The Dhammapada – The Path of Perfection*.

Create an 'inspiration board' at home. Pin up and attach things that you find inspiring – anything at all from cards to labels to leaves!

Find out where the highest natural point in your county is and (as long as it's not dangerous!) visit it to experience the view.

Hire a fancy dress costume and wear it out with your friends.

Design your own board game – why not invite some friends around to play it with you?

Go along to a protest march and soak up some of the passion and emotion. Alternatively, why not start a petition of your own?

If you see a recipe on a cooking show or in the newspaper that gets your mouth watering, get down to the supermarket, find the ingredients and start cooking!

Go to the insect house at your local zoo, or natural history museum, and watch the way that leafcutter ants work together to achieve their goal.

What you are will show in what you do.

Thomas Edison

One is not born a genius, one becomes a genius.

Simone De Beauvoir

Spend an evening at a restaurant you've never been to before – and order something you wouldn't usually eat.

Create a piece of 'cut-up' writing. Collect single pages from different newspapers, magazines and other publications; cut each page into four and then mix and match the quarters to create new sentences.

Try to write a song using only three notes.

Draw yourself as a character from *The Lord of the Rings*.

18 Decorate your desk at work or at home with pictures of people or places that inspire you, calm you or motivate you.

19 Take up a pub game – darts, dominoes, cribbage, bar billiards. If you find you enjoy it, search for a local team or league nearby.

20 Recreate a scene from a favourite film or novel – swinging around lampposts in the pouring rain or hijacking the mic on a parade float to sing 'Twist and Shout'.

Every artist was first an amateur.

Ralph Waldo Emerson

The power of imagination makes us infinite.

John Muir

Get down to your local park or playing field for some outdoor sporting fun!

Gaze out across a pond or stream and watch the way the fish, dragonflies and water boatmen affect the water's surface.

Spend a few minutes slowly crafting the perfect sentence. It could be about the emotions you're feeling right now, your favourite season, the taste of your morning coffee… anything.

Be a tourist in your own town: go to the Tourist Information office, pick up leaflets, and go sightseeing!

Go to the beach and dig your toes into the sand. Listen to the waves on the shore. Think about the colour of the sea, the taste of the salty air. Think of one word which perfectly sums up what your senses are experiencing.

Design a comic book cover that imagines you and your friends as superheroes.

Go to a car boot sale or charity shop and buy a cheap guitar or keyboard. Even if you have never played before, make up a song.

Sleep outside under the open sky.

Make a fruit salad using no less than eight different fruits – try adding a dash of Grand Marnier to give it a bit of oomph!

AUGUST

Send a message in a bottle.

Throw a holiday-themed garden party. Decorate your garden, invite your guests to dress up, and play some fitting music. Nibbles and drinks must match the theme too!

Find an indoor ski slope or ice-skating rink and remember what winter feels like.

Try learning a new language. Download an app or buy a 'teach yourself' book, and commit to learning five new words or phrases per day.

Make your own ice lollies using only natural ingredients – or have a go at ice-cream if you're feeling adventurous.

World Meditation Day: Find a meditation workshop event near you and give it a try.

Wear 1920s-style clothes to work.

Visit a bookshop and select a book at random – buy it and read it from cover to cover.

Organise a water-pistol war with friends – don't forget balloons for water bombs!

Think of one thing that would make a big change in your work life and drop it in your suggestion box. If your workplace doesn't have one, suggest that you get one!

It is never too late to be what you might have been.

George Eliot

Poetry is the one place where people can speak their original human mind.

Allen Ginsberg

International Left-Handers Day: Try contour drawing (drawing without looking at the paper) with the opposite hand to the one you usually use – it might not look like much but it'll be fun!

Buy a yo-yo and aim to learn at least five tricks.

Watch an outdoor performance – there are always classical concerts or Shakespeare performances at this time of year.

Go boating – on a canal, river, lake or at the sea side, whatever you fancy.

Do one good deed today.

Walk or cycle slowly down a road and imagine who lives in each house. Create a dramatic story for each one – a secret addiction, a love affair or some literal skeletons in closets!

Think about your home and how you could make it greener – whether by simply unplugging all your electronic appliances when they're not in use or investing in solar panels.

My heart leaps up when I behold
A rainbow in the sky:
So was it when my life began,
So is it now I am a man…

William Wordsworth

It is in vain to say that human beings ought to be satisfied with tranquillity: they must have action; and they will make it if they cannot find it.

Charlotte Brontë

Find a piece of art, literature or music that is as least 2,000 years old, and create its modern counterpart.

Try going through the weekend without checking the time – ignore your clock/watch/phone and simply act on impulse.

Start a family tree using photos of your relatives – or, if you're short on photos, why not draw your family members?

Look outside and count how many different shades and colours you can see. Think of the perfect word to describe each tone: olive, pistachio, lawn green, jungle green, mint, chartreuse.

Do something you haven't done since you were a child – climb a tree, play with a ball, go on a bike ride to the park.

Create some quirky and original book-ends out of found objects you have (and if you don't have any, start looking!).

Go outside and photograph at least five different animals.

Draw an object you look at every day, such as a Marmite jar, your handbag or your overflowing chest of drawers. Draw every detail, taking your time.

Read as many poems as you can today. Try to find one poem which perfectly summarises your mood right now.

SEPTEMBER

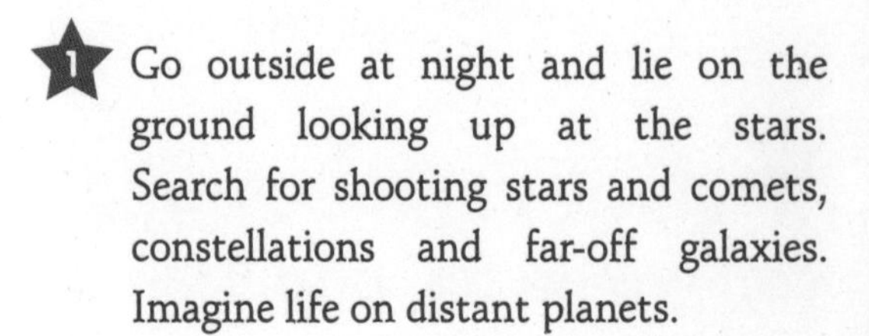

1. Go outside at night and lie on the ground looking up at the stars. Search for shooting stars and comets, constellations and far-off galaxies. Imagine life on distant planets.

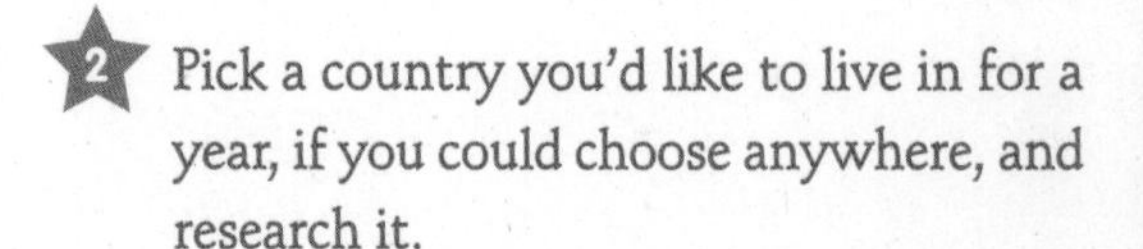

2. Pick a country you'd like to live in for a year, if you could choose anywhere, and research it.

First say to yourself what you would be; and then do what you have to do.

Epictetus

A wise man will make more opportunities than he finds.

Francis Bacon

Switch on the radio and have some fun by singing along with alternative lyrics.

Make a Green Man for your garden out of clay or supple twigs. If you don't have a garden, make one for your local park.

Read a classic novel that you never thought you'd get round to reading.

Create a piece of Banksy-style street art using a stencil, spray paint and a large canvas.

Organise a regular movie night with friends, where you each choose and watch your top three films by your favourite actor (one each night).

Recreate the 'blind dining' experience at home – eat in the dark, so that your other senses are heightened.

Immerse yourself in a virtual fantasy world by signing up for an online role-playing game.

Mindfulness Day: Close your eyes and breathe as slowly as possible. Become aware of all the things you can feel: the weight of your body on your chair, your hair against your forehead, a slight breeze through a window.

International Chocolate Day: Look for a new recipe involving chocolate and cook two batches – one to give away and one to keep!

Volunteer to help tend the grounds at your local park or communal garden.

Use a photo-editing computer program to transform your portrait into something silly and outrageous – give yourself a new hair style, funny accessories, etc. Or simply get a print of your photo and doodle over it.

Flick through today's paper and cut out words or phrases that strike you as interesting. Arrange your words and phrases to make a statement or poem.

Go to see the original of your favourite painting in an art gallery, if you can, to see how different it looks in reality as opposed to as a print.

Enjoy the little things, for one day you may look back and realise they were the big things.

Robert Brault

The more you lose yourself in something bigger than yourself, the more energy you will have.

Norman Peale

Play – hide-and-seek, hopscotch, tag…

International Day of Peace: Consider these words from the Dalai Lama: 'We can never obtain peace in the outer world until we make peace with ourselves.'

Take a duvet day or unscheduled holiday and spend the day doing absolutely nothing at all!

Make or design a piece of jewellery for someone you love.

Use aural stimuli to help you with your work. Try listening to sound effects such as a rough, crashing sea or birds twittering (you can find them online) before you get going.

Dig out your school yearbook or report book and think about how you have changed – and how you have stayed the same.

Try your hand at writing a children's story – you could even add your own illustrations if you feel up to it.

Make bunting and use it to decorate your garden or the front of your home.

Research the history of your hometown. Find out about any local myths or legends.

Go to a jazz or swing club and soak up the atmosphere.

Experiment with making your own cocktail – think about your favourite alcoholic drink, your favourite fruits and soft drinks and see what you come up with!

OCTOBER

Create a scrapbook to document your day – keep your receipts, tickets, wrappers and other bits and pieces you encounter and put them together on a page in the book.

Buy frames for your favourite photos and arrange them on one large wall in your home. Or if you have lots of little snapshots, pin them to the biggest cork board you can get your hands on.

… sooner or later,
the man who wins
Is the man who thinks he can.

Walter D. Wintle

Some are born great, some achieve greatness, and some have greatness thrust upon 'em.

William Shakespeare, *Twelfth Night*

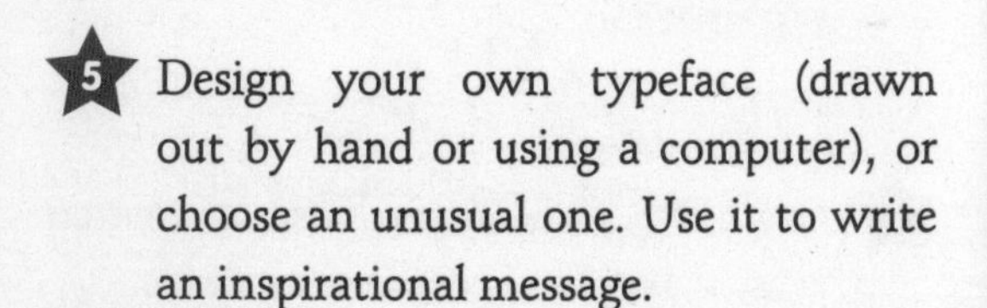

5 Design your own typeface (drawn out by hand or using a computer), or choose an unusual one. Use it to write an inspirational message.

6 Read a book set in a country you've never visited.

7 Challenge someone to a game of chess – you can play online if you don't have a board. If you don't know how to play, use today to learn.

Try a type of tea that you've never tasted before.

Get lost. Walk down an unexplored road or path and see where it leads.

Go to an online photo-sharing website and find three photos which grab your attention. Next, try to form a story from the photos.

Research a company or organisation that interests you. Read their mission statement and learn about their values and ethics.

Buy a Dictaphone and record the sounds of your day.

Rent a cottage in the countryside, preferably one with a real log fire, and escape there for a night or two with a pile of good books and a bottle of wine. Don't forget to take a cosy jumper!

Dance around your front room like a madman when nobody's watching.

Go to a life-drawing class with a friend.

Buy a small-sized, plain paper notebook and create a flip-page animation of something that makes you smile. Keep it in your pocket for when you need cheering up.

Read *The Diving Bell and the Butterfly* by Jean-Dominique Bauby and reflect on the things we take for granted.

The pessimist sees difficulty in every opportunity. The optimist sees the opportunity in every difficulty.

Winston Churchill

I write when I'm inspired, and I see to it that I'm inspired at 9.00 every morning.

Peter de Vries

20 Find a food shop you don't usually go to and browse for inspiration – or even better, do your weekly shop there!

21

Apple Day: Go scrumping, and bake a pie or cake with the goods.

22 Take a CD at random off your shelf (or hit shuffle on your computer) and skip to the last line of the last track. Use this line as inspiration for a piece of writing, perhaps as a title or a first line.

Revisit the neighbourhood in which you grew up. Take an hour or two to wander around and soak up the memories.

Fill one side of A4 paper with your argument for something you feel passionately about. Fill the other side with the strongest counter-argument you can think of.

Find a recipe for pumpkin soup, or pumpkin pie, and give it a try.

Gulliver's Travels was published this day in 1726: spend the day imagining how life would be if you were really tiny or if everything else had shrunk.

Draw something with a Sharpie pen.

Ask a parent to describe the events leading up to and immediately after your birth. Write about it as if you were a fly on the wall.

Is there a type of dance you've always admired? Look into classes now.

Imagine and draw your own vehicle.

Halloween: Try your hand at pumpkin carving – don't just stick to scary faces, try carving out cats, witches, bats and other spooky silhouettes.

NOVEMBER

Revisit an animated cartoon series you enjoyed as a child.

Wear something yellow today – it will make you happy!

Imagine yourself as a cat or a dog – what kind would you be? Draw or write about it.

Try to go a whole day without saying anything negative.

Bonfire Night: Go to the top of the highest hill around and watch the magnificent displays from up above.

Research and construct a 'dream machine' for yourself (a home-made flicker lamp which produces silhouettes that stimulate your optical senses).

The future belongs to the few of us still willing to get our hands dirty.

Roland Tiangco

You can't use up creativity. The more you use, the more you have.

Maya Angelou

Try being creative with wool – knit a winter scarf, hat or tea cosy.

Make a list of the personal values and character traits that are most important to you.

Light a candle and focus on the movement of the flame and the quality of the light. Allow yourself to just be still and quiet, for as long as you like. Enjoy the silence.

Visit your local library and go to a section you'd never think to look at.

Write a letter to yourself five years ago, or five years in the future. Tell yourself things you wished you'd known or things you hope to remember.

Make your own Christmas cards.

It's not where you take things from, it's where you take them to.

Jean-Luc Godard

If at first the idea is not absurd, then there is no hope for it.

Albert Einstein

Find a picture you like. Turn it upside down, and try to copy it. You'll be surprised how differently you look at things when viewing them from a new angle.

Read a novel in a day. Preferably curled up on a sofa with a supply of your favourite brew and biscuits.

International Men's Day: Think about a man in your life who you admire. Visualise his face, think about his attitude and his body language and work out what it is about him that makes him great.

Write a story that is exactly 100 words long.

Buy a pack of blank postcards. Doodle, paint or stamp designs on the fronts of all of them, write your favourite inspirational quote on the back, and send them to all your favourite people.

Download an interesting debate on a podcast or a talk from TED (Technology, Entertainment and Design) and listen to it on your commute. Try to take in as much of the discussion as possible.

Create your own design for the cover of one of your favourite albums.

Buy yourself a set of weights (even if they are the light ones!) and commit to doing a certain number of reps every day.

Think of two words that you suspect nobody has ever put together before, such as 'crunchy aerobics' or 'salamander pancakes'.

Cook a meal that includes all of your five-a-day fruit and/or vegetables.

Write down one major change you want to make. See if you can break it down into three smaller, more realistic changes. Now break one of those down even further and make one of those changes today.

Go out and pick some sloes to make sloe gin.

Buy a paper and don't put it down until you've solved the 'challenging' crossword or Sudoku all by yourself.

Listen to a composition by Mozart – he inspired Albert Einstein, and he may inspire you too!

DECEMBER

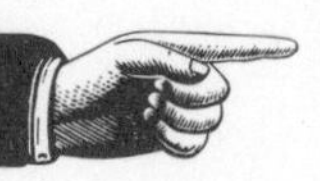

1. Get out of a rut: shake up your daily routine by having lunch in a new spot, or with a different colleague.

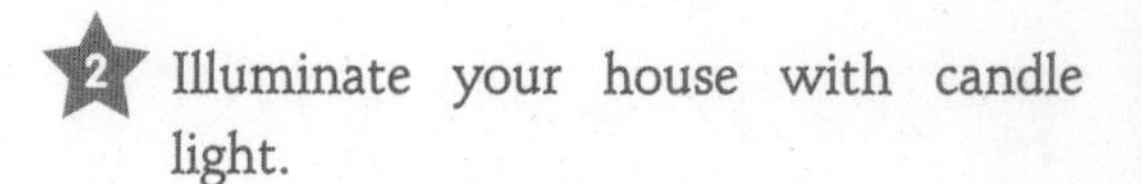

2. Illuminate your house with candle light.

3. Fill an entire A4 sheet by drawing colourful patterns or motifs – make them as simple or as complicated as you like.

The longer you wait for the future, the shorter it will be.

Loesje slogan

Anything Anytime Anyplace For No Reason At All.

Frank Zappa

Smile at everyone you pass for the day, and notice how it affects the way you feel.

Watch a classic black-and-white film and notice the artistry in the cinematography.

Pay a surprise visit to a friend or relative you haven't seen in a while, and take them a Christmas pudding or mince pies.

Lie down, close your eyes, and visualise every step of a journey you once made and would like to recall. Remember the smells and sounds you encountered.

Treat yourself to a long bubble bath, complete with candles and some relaxing music in the background. Let your mind wander.

Plan out the screenplay for the film of your life so far. Work out which actors will play all the main parts.

Either you run the day or the day runs you.

Jim Rohn

Aim for the moon. If you miss, you may hit a star.

W. Clement Stone

 Go to a ballet or opera performance – there are lots of companies with touring performances of *The Nutcracker* at this time of year!

 Make presents for your closest friends or family: jewellery, a decorated photo frame or a scrapbook of memories, or try something more unusual like candle- or soap-making.

 Make gingerbread and decorate it with snowy-white icing.

Book a last-minute flight online and see how they celebrate Yuletide in a different part of the world.

Compose your own seasonal carol – either a classic to go down in history or a comedy attempt only fit to be sung to your friends!

Have a go at making your own festive decorations out of odds and ends you have in the house – fabric from old clothes, paint from half-empty cans – and things you can collect from your garden or a park – pine cones, twigs, holly.

Read something by Charles Dickens, such as *Great Expectations* or *A Christmas Carol.*

Winter Solstice: Invite all your friends over, put on some classic tunes, indulge in too much chocolate and brandy and make the most of the shortest day of the year!

Design your own movie poster – it could be for a made-up film or one of your all-time favourites.

Make mulled wine from fresh fruit, spices and red wine.

Attend a holiday celebration at a local pub or bar.

Christmas Day: Make a conscious effort not to overdo it with food and drink. The festive season is about being good to each other – and yourself!

Boxing Day: Spring a surprise visit on a friend or relative who is spending the festive period alone – make it interesting by walking there.

Think of an activity you can share with your family (aside from watching TV!) and do your best to convince them all to take part.

Decorate a shoe box with leftover wrapping paper and use it to store all your Christmas cards once you've taken them down.

Design and make thank you cards for all the people you saw or received gifts from over the festive period.

Turn back to 1 January in your journal, and reflect on how your thoughts, actions and talents have changed over the year.

A truly good book teaches me better than to read it. I must soon lay it down, and commence living on its hint. What I began by reading, I must finish by acting.

Henry David Thoreau